Our Mothers' Recipes

Remembering the meals that shaped our lives

Jonathan Cutler and Lanny Udell

GWHIZZ BOOKS

ISBN: 0-9713139-1-1
Published by:
GWhizz Books
38 Miller Avenue, PMB 129
Mill Valley, CA 94941
www.gwhizzbooks.com

First printing: March 2002
Printed and bound by Hignell Printing, Ltd., Winnipeg, Manitoba, Canada

<u>Acknowledgements</u>

Special thanks to

all our contributors, because really…this is their book.

To Ginny Walters of GWhizz Books for her good advice, and for believing in us.

And to Joe Loconto, our most talented graphic designer

who has gone above and beyond the call of duty.

Growing up in the 40's, 50's or early 60's had a flavor all its own. In the days before food processors, microwaves and bread machines, our mothers prepared simple, honest, tasty meals that satisfied our deepest needs.

When we began talking to people…drawing them out about their mother's cooking…their memories fell into two distinct camps. Most fondly recalled the indelible tastes and aromas of their youth. Then there was the other camp. As one friend put it, "Are you kidding? Dinner at our house was three blobs on a plate."

Food is a little like music in its emotional power. Spin a Paul Anka tune or listen to Sinatra, and you're instantly transported back in time. Think of mom's meatloaf or her creamy chocolate pudding, and the memories come rushing right back. Vivid images like, "The fragrant smell of her sauce bubbling on the stove…filled the house and made my mouth water." Or, "I'd sneak down to the kitchen early in the morning and snitch a slice of that lemon meringue pie before I went to school, hoping my mother wouldn't notice."

For the most part, our moms cooked intuitively, seasoning, tasting and adding ingredients as they went along. In some families, grandma ruled the range, and in others it was dad who stepped up to the plate. But no matter who it was, we found that one thing is universally true: Food equals love. As one contributor wrote, there was "Lots of talking and laughter, hugging and kissing. Everyone just waited for the lid to come off the pot and that heavenly aroma to waft through the house."

So it seems that our connection to the past is inextricably linked to the foods we loved as kids. Now, many of our mothers' recipes, whether actually written or taught by example, live on to nourish the next generation. The recipes and recollections served up here are arranged randomly, as memories often are, and they're offered as a loving tribute to all those who fed and nurtured us.

One of our contributors may have summed it up best when she wrote of her mother, "Her love, a flavor that only she was able to produce, made my life delicious in many ways. Food was just one of them."

JC & LU

PS—We've left a few blank pages at the back of the book for you to add your own recipes, photos and recollections.

I don't have many childhood memories that don't include a table heaped with food. This is where we'd share our day…eating, laughing, crying, debating…and eating. Unusual for the 50's, my mom worked from 9 to 5, but by 6 pm she had a hot dinner on the table.

What I remember most were Sunday feasts. This meal almost always included pasta. It could be spaghetti, lasagna, ravioli or gnocchi, but it was the fragrant smell of her sauce bubbling on the stove that filled the house and made my mouth water. I can follow her sauce recipe to the letter and it still doesn't taste the same. It's only now, after years of trying to duplicate it, that I realize I never will.

Her secret ingredient was hers alone. It enhanced everything in my life. Her love, a flavor that only she was able to produce, made my life delicious in many ways. Food was just one of them.

—From her daughter Carol McBurnie

Vera Muelli's Spaghetti Sauce

2 cloves garlic (more if desired)

2-3 tbsp olive oil

1 lb veal stew or lean pork (meat can be removed once sauce is done and served as a side dish)

1 small onion, optional

Oregano, basil (approx. 1 tbsp of each, or to taste)

1 or 2 bay leaves

Salt

Sugar

2 28-oz cans crushed tomatoes

1 32-oz can tomato juice

In a large pot, brown the garlic to golden, then remove and set aside. Add chopped onion and cook until soft. Add meat, brown completely but not too dark. Add tomatoes, juice and seasonings and stir. Bring to boil then reduce heat to low. Simmer for approx. 1 hour adding salt to taste, and sugar if you want the sauce to be sweeter. Those two little pieces of garlic can now be crushed and added back into the sauce. You can also add browned meatballs or sausage...everything you put in the sauce will add flavor.

The longer you cook the sauce uncovered, the thicker it will become as it cooks down. Remove bay leaves before serving. Leftover sauce can be frozen. Enjoy!

It was the early 1950's, and each summer my family rented a small bungalow on the Jersey shore for the last two weeks of August. My uncle had an 18-foot sailboat that we dragged with us via a homemade trailer. The highlight of the vacation was the clamming trip. It took us two hours of sailing to get to the inlet where the clams were the biggest. My uncle would find a shallow spot and we would leap off the boat into waist-high water. He used a rake to find the clams, but my brother and I used our toes. It took us the whole afternoon to harvest a bushel of nice large clams, and then we were back on the boat for the long sail home, tired and sunburned.

My uncle shucked the clams on the dock and my mother put them in a large pot she had brought along for just that reason. All the other ingredients had been prepared ahead of time.

My mother added the fresh clams and within an hour we were enjoying the secret family recipe that had been passed down from mother to daughter for generations.

—From her son Richard Voehl

Midge Voehl's Clam Pie

Pastry for 2-crust 9" or 10" pie
Piece of salt pork (about 2" x 3")
2 doz large clams, open and save juice
2 large potatoes, peeled and diced
3 large onions, sliced
Few saltines or Uneeda biscuits, crushed

Dice and cook salt pork in 6 cups of water at a low boil until tender, approx. 30 min. Grind clam meat and salt pork in meat grinder. Add potatoes and onions to salt pork water and cook until tender but not mushy. Add the ground clams, clam juice and salt pork last 10 min. Season with salt and pepper to taste.

With slotted spoon, lift pie filling from cooking pot and layer in pie shell, spreading cracker crumbs between 2 or 3 layers to bind filling together. Add top crust and make slits to let steam escape. Bake at 450° for 10 min. then lower heat to 350° and bake about 40 min. or till nicely browned. Thicken liquid in pot with a flour and butter roux and use as gravy or "dip" over wedge shaped pieces of pie.

My mother, Josephine Roth, grew up in Chicago and was of Hungarian descent. Mom was a wonderful cook. Not only were her meals delicious, but she was an accomplished baker as well. In fact, throughout my childhood, from the time I went to summer camp and all through college, I knew I could count on her cookies showing up in the mail on a regular basis. Sometimes she'd pack them in a shoebox, other times they'd arrive nestled in a one-pound coffee tin which she requested that I return so she could use it again—an early instance of recycling. I was, of course, happy to oblige.

Nothing brought her greater joy than to give baking lessons to family—particularly granddaughters—and friends. Sadly, my mother passed away in 1996, but her baking tradition lives on as my daughter Sarah has built her own successful cookie company, Sarah Bear Cookies.

—From her son Phil Roth

Josephine Roth's Pogacsa
(Hungarian Cookies)

4 cups flour, sifted
1 cup sugar
2 tsp baking powder
1 tsp salt
2 sticks margarine
1 small can Carnation milk
4 egg yolks, beaten
1 1/2 tsp vanilla

Using a slotted spoon, combine first four ingredients in a large bowl.
Cut in the 2 sticks of margarine.
In one-cup measuring receptacle, combine the milk, eggs yolks and vanilla.
Stir into dry ingredients and mix well.

Divide dough into four sections and roll out on board. Cut with small glass dipped in flour.
Brush tops with egg yolk mixed with 1 tbsp milk. Bake at 375° about 15 minutes.

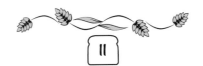

When I was married in 1965, I was given a surprise bridal shower. Each guest was asked to bring a favorite recipe to start me on my way as a married woman and good housekeeper. In my family, good cooking was an important part of "good housekeeping." For me, it was never a chore because I had the memory of a kitchen full of the quick hands and laughter that was generated whenever my mother and her four sisters, first generation Italian women, came together to create a joyous family feast.

My mother brought her lasagna recipe—one of my favorites—to the shower. It was usually served as an everyday meal with fresh-cut vegetables and garlic bread made with sweet Italian crusted bread. It was standard fare at our house, and only now do I begin to appreciate the time and love that was poured into her "simple" meals.

—From her daughter Jacky Dana

Mary Chimento-Kamp's Lasagna

1 to 1 1/2 pkg of lasagna noodles
1 onion, chopped
2 cans tomato paste
2 cups water
Salt and pepper
Garlic powder

Italian seasoning
3/4 cup sliced mushrooms
1 lb ground chuck or Italian sausage
1 to 1 1/2 cups cottage cheese
3/4 lb mozzarella or Monterey Jack cheese
Grated Parmesan cheese

Brown the meat with the onions. Add the mushrooms,
seasonings, tomato paste and water. Cook long and slow.

Boil lasagna noodles and drain.
Place a thin layer of sauce in a 9"x 12" baking dish.
Arrange lasagna in layers alternately with layers of sauce, mozzarella and cottage cheese.
Sprinkle with grated Parmesan cheese. Bake at 350° for 20 minutes or until heated through
and mozzarella is melted.

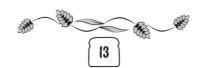

My mother always said she wasn't a great cook. But I thought she was. Maybe it's because her mother had once operated a small restaurant in San Francisco's Old Jewish neighborhood. Or maybe it's because our Dad was such a picky eater.

Pearl's kitchen always smelled wonderful. The aromas of chicken soup, meatloaf and blintzes would waft through our house. But when she baked up her signature dish of Pineapple Chicken, we'd toss our homework on the floor and make a bee line for the dinner table.

The mixture of sweet pineapple with tart green peppers and tender chicken would just melt in your mouth. It was a dish she always served to special company.

—From her son Gil Zeimer

Pearl Zeimer's Pineapple Chicken

2 fryers, cut up
Flour
Salt and pepper

Paprika
1 stick butter
1/2 cup vegetable oil

For Sauce:

1 cup Sherry
1/2 cup brown sugar
2 cans pineapple chunks with juice

4 sliced scallions
1 large diced green pepper
1 package slivered almonds

Preheat oven to 425°

Mix chicken parts in bag with flour, salt, pepper and paprika. Melt butter with oil in baking dish in oven. Add chicken skin side down. Bake at 425° for 30 minutes.

Turn chicken over and turn oven down to 375°. In a bowl, mix together sauce ingredients and pour over chicken. Sprinkle slivered almonds on top. Bake for another 40 minutes, basting every 15 minutes. Serves 8 to 10.

What I remember most about my mother's cooking is that she played it by ear, not to mention by mouth and nose. Though she'd sometimes consult a handwritten recipe, one she'd either written for herself in years past or had received from a friend, most of the time it seemed an instinctual process.

The Better Homes & Gardens cookbook languished on a nearby kitchen shelf, infrequently opened, except perhaps to stuff a newly written recipe between its leaves. Mom had obviously learned from watching her mother cook, an on-the-job apprenticeship as old as kitchens. She'd add one ingredient after another, tasting between each, and the result was inevitably sublime.

—From her son Robert Fliegel

Aileene Fliegel's Chocolate Fudge Brownies

3/4 cup sifted cake flour
1/2 tsp baking powder
1/3 cup butter
2 squares bitter chocolate, melted
1 cup sugar
2 eggs, well beaten
1 tsp vanilla
1/2 cup nuts

Sift flour once, measure, add baking powder and sift again.
Add butter to chocolate and blend. Combine sugar and eggs.
Add chocolate mixture, beat in thoroughly the flour, vanilla, and nuts.
Pour into greased square pan and bake at 350° for 35 minutes.
Cut in squares before removing from pan.

Fancier families may have called this Beef Burgundy, but in our circle of family and friends it was just "Marge's Beef and Noodles"…and no one ever turned down an invitation when the call went out. I can still see everyone milling around the table nibbling on chips and dip and drinking highballs while mom simmered her stew, baked a loaf or two of bread and threw together a salad.

Lots of talking and laughter, hugging and kissing. After all, we were German Irish Catholics, so life was never expected to be less than festive chaos. Kids set the table and fetched the drinks. Glen Miller serenaded in the background. Everyone just waited for the lid to come off the pot, and that heavenly aroma to waft through the house. Most of all I remember after dinner, people with spoons and bits of bread hovered around the stove vying for the last of the beef and noodles, mopping up the last of the scrumptious gravy.

Mom always used to say it was even better the second day, though how she came to that conclusion remains a mystery!

—From her daughter Lynn Winter

Marjorie Schmieman's Beef and Noodles

3 lbs cubed sirloin
Butter for browning
1/2 cup beef broth
Pepper and salt to taste
4 tbsp butter
1/3 cup flour

2 1/2 cups Burgundy
6 oz salt pork
18 boiling onions
1/2 stick butter
1 lb fresh mushrooms

In a heavy roasting pan, quickly brown the beef cubes in a small amount of butter. Pour off excess fat and replace it with the beef broth. Salt lightly, add pepper to taste. Cover the pan tightly and simmer.

Sauce: Melt 4 tbsp butter, add the flour, stirring constantly, and cook to a golden yellow. Add wine a little at a time, and allow it to stand on low heat for 45 minutes. Pour the sauce over the beef and simmer gently for 3 1/2 hours on top of the stove or in the oven at 300°.

Cut salt pork into little cubes and brown them in butter. Add the onions and simmer for 1 1/2 hours. Add to the meat one hour before serving. Melt 1/2 stick of butter over medium heat in a skillet. When the foam subsides, add the mushrooms and toss until soft. Combine the mushrooms with the beef and onions 15 minutes before serving.

Serve over generous portions of wide noodles, butter and fresh snipped parsley optional. Serves 8

Casting a line into a wild stream was a lifelong mania of my dad's. After he married my mom in California, he swept her off to his native Colorado where he introduced her to his family and showed her his favorite childhood fishing spots.

Over the years my dad's fishing trips yielded hundreds of memorable meals for family and friends, and his pan fried fish became legendary.

He delighted in preparing it in his own special way, developed through trial and error. When I married and set up a household of my own, I panicked the first time I tried to recreate my dad's fish recipe. Not recalling the exact process, my fish began to experience problems. I quickly got on the phone to dad. Pencil in hand, I took careful notes as he walked me through his tried and true method.

Dad's secret for pan frying delicate fish like bass, trout and catfish produces a crisp and succulent result that retains just the right firmness. I might add that he enjoyed stirring up his special martini while he had the fish resting in its egg bath.

—From his daughter Cathy Shea

Marko Lee Green's Pan Fried Fish Filet

3 to 4 lbs bass, catfish or trout filet, cut into 3" to 4" lengths
1 cup seasoned breadcrumbs, preferably Contadina brand
1/2 tsp Schilling Seasoned Salt
1/2 tsp garlic powder
Black pepper to taste
2 eggs
1/2 cup cooking oil (Saffola or Canola preferred)

Combine Seasoned Salt, garlic powder and black pepper with breadcrumbs and set aside. Have a large plate or waxed paper ready to hold the breadcrumb mixture for coating fish. Beat eggs until mixed well (don't add milk or water to eggs as this will cause the fish to get soggy in the frying pan). Rinse filets in ice water and pat dry. Soak filets in beaten eggs for 15 to 20 minutes. About 5 minutes before the fish is ready to come out of the egg, heat the oil in a large skillet until it is just ready to smoke (about 375°). Coat fish in breadcrumb mixture and place in skillet. Fry until golden, 3 to 5 minutes on each side, turning once.

Optional:
While the fish is soaking in the egg, place 5 ice cubes and 1 jalapeno-stuffed green olive in an old-fashion glass. Pour in 2 jiggers of vodka (Smirnoff was my dad's usual). Add a splash of dry vermouth and a dash of the olive juice. Stir exactly 21 times, as prescribed by Ian Fleming for James Bond. Serve immediately.

One of my fondest childhood memories is hurrying home from school to see what delicious delight would be waiting for me. Most days, there was the aroma of freshly baked bread wafting from the kitchen (my mom baked five loaves every week), and I never knew when I would arrive home to find fresh-

baked cinnamon rolls or my favorite, her Lazy Day Muffins. More often than not, my friends would tag along, just hoping they had hit the jackpot and it would be baking day.

Mom always saved enough dough so we could have warm rolls with dinner or cinnamon buns for dessert. And sometimes she made fried bread, which I never figured out how to make. We would sprinkle powdered sugar on top or just have it with butter and jam. What a treat! Mom kept her bread recipes in her head, but I did manage to copy down her muffin recipe, and now, every time I make them, the scents and emotions of my childhood come flooding back.

—From her daughter Linda Gattuccio

Evelyn Brown's Lazy Day Muffins

1 cup All Bran cereal
1 cup boiling water
2 1/4 cups flour
2 1/4 tsp baking soda
1 tsp salt

2 1/2 cups bran flakes
1/2 cup oil
1 1/2 cups sugar
2 eggs
1/2 qt buttermilk

Preheat oven to 400°

Pour boiling water over All Bran and set aside. Combine flour, baking soda, salt and bran flakes.
Mix sugar into oil and beat in eggs, then add the buttermilk. Mix in bran/water mixture and stir
to blend, gradually adding the flour mixture until smooth.

Fill muffin tins 2/3 full and bake at 400° for approximately 20 minutes.
Muffins will last up to 2 weeks covered and refrigerated.

My grandmother grew up in Thief River Falls, Minnesota. She moved to Minneapolis in the 1920's with her husband Frank, and their son (my dad), Emery. Typical of the time, Grandma had a special day dedicated to certain tasks...Monday was laundry day, on Tuesday she ironed, etc. Of course, my favorite day to visit was Friday, baking day, when there were always cinnamon rolls, homemade bread and cookies, fresh from the oven.

I have wonderful memories of Thanksgiving dinners at my grandparents' house. Grandma would prepare a traditional meal with all the trimmings. The turkey went into the oven the night before and roasted, slowly, overnight at a low temperature so it was always tender and juicy. But my fondest memory is her Candlelight Salad.

When the family gathered at the table, inevitably someone would bump it pulling up their chair and some of the salads would topple over, sending the cherries rolling in every direction. In talking with my relatives in later years, I realized that we all thought this was normal, and none of us ever saw the humor in it until we were grown up!

—From her granddaughter Nanci Shapiro

Hulda Myrold Erickson's Candlelight Salad

Iceberg lettuce
Canned pineapple rings
Bananas
Maraschino cherries

Place 1 iceberg lettuce leaf on a salad plate to make a bed.
Then, put 1 pineapple ring on top of the lettuce.
Stand 1/2 banana upright in the hole of the pineapple ring.
Add a maraschino cherry on top of the banana to look like the candle flame.

(You may have to cut a notch in the banana for the cherry to sit on,
or use a toothpick to stick it on.)

My mom was raised in upstate New York. Her grandmother had a farm at the end of the streetcar line, and mom remembers going there when all her cousins, aunts and uncles would congregate. They would move the furniture out of the way, sing, play music and dance. It was at the farm that mom learned to cook. To her, food was love, and one of her greatest joys was preparing a beautiful, delicious meal for friends and relatives. Everyone looked forward to an invitation to the O'Connell's house for dinner.

I remember one Thanksgiving when a total stranger came to dinner. It seems that Mom and Dad had met him at a restaurant in town and he didn't have anyplace to go for the holiday. So naturally, Mom invited him!

It is hard for me to imagine myself being as open and innocent as my mother was in those days. Today at 83, having survived the deaths of two husbands and one child, she is a woman of great goodness and much wisdom, always willing to help a neighbor or be a friend.

—From her daughter Morgan Dill

Eleanor Ann O'Connell's Pot Roast

3-4 lb tri-tip roast
Lawry's Seasoned Salt
Black pepper
Flour
Thyme
2 tbsp Lea & Perrins Worcestershire Sauce
2 tbsp soy sauce
1/4 cup wine
1 small onion, cut up
2 cloves of garlic put thru garlic press

Put roast, fat side down, in Dutch oven over low heat. (If there's not much fat on the roast, add a little olive oil). After you have 2 tbsp of fat in the pan, brown the meat on all sides, slowly. Sprinkle with Lawry's Seasoned Salt and black pepper.

Remove meat from pan and dredge in flour. Return to pan and add Worcestershire Sauce, soy sauce, wine, onion, and garlic. Add a little water if necessary. Sprinkle a little more pepper and some thyme on roast. Cook in 300° oven until tender. Add more water during cooking if gravy becomes too thick. Meat is done when it easily falls off when pierced with a fork.

Mom was a small town gal and moved to the big city (Brooklyn, NY) when she married my Dad. She was a simple woman with simple needs, and her life revolved around family and food. When they were first married Mom didn't know how to cook, as evidenced by this anecdote that Dad loved to tell. One day he came home from work and found Mom crying. She had tried to make Jello but it didn't 'jell'. Dad, seeing the Jello standing on the counter, asked her how long it had been in the refrigerator, at which point she began to cry louder. You see, she hadn't put the Jello in the refrigerator at all!

In time, Mom's cooking abilitiy improved greatly. Some of her delicious recipes included rugalach, stuffed cabbage, sour cream cake, chocolate cake, sponge cake and, last but not least, her famous sweet potatoes in corn flakes. Even when she could no longer cook an entire holiday meal, we all insisted that she just make the potatoes. Needless to say, I miss her.

—From her daughter Rhonda Plawner

Millie Kaplan's Sweet Potatoes in Corn Flakes

6 sweet potatoes
Salt to taste
1 egg
1/4 cup matzo meal
1/4 cup orange juice
Corn flakes
Oil for frying

Put potatoes in a pot of cold water. Add some salt. Cover and
boil until skin is soft, about 1/2 hour. Spill off water and allow to cool.
Peel then mash in a mixing bowl with egg and salt. Add the matzo meal and orange juice.
Mix thoroughly.

Place corn flakes in a pie plate. Shape potato mixture into patties and roll them in the corn
flakes. Fry in hot oil about 5 minutes on each side. Drain and serve.

Ah, sponge cake! Light and fluffy, sweet and yellow. This was one of my mother's specialties. And when the rich, citrus-y aroma began to emanate from the kitchen, it meant company was coming.

My sister and I would race into the kitchen and see the tall metal cake pan perched upside down on the neck of a wine bottle, the traditional way this cake cooled. Then came the unveiling, and "the taste." My mother always took a proprietary taste before anyone else, just to make sure it was good enough to serve. Then she'd relinquish the pan to our waiting fingers, and we'd scrape it clean, eating the crumbs since the cake was "for company."

One time, though, the cake didn't rise. Instead of the tall, golden top cresting the pan, there was a crumpled, wrinkly brown cake only half the proper height. There was nothing to do but start over. We all tiptoed around the house, fearing that the slightest movement might make the cake fall. We weren't as upset by this as my mother, because guess who got to eat the cake that wasn't good enough for company?

—*From her daughter Phyllis Evans*

Ethel Jaffe's Sponge Cake

10 large eggs
2 cups sugar
Juice of 1 fresh orange and 1 small lemon
2 cups cake flour (measure after sifting)
2 level tsp baking powder
1/4 tsp salt

Separate the eggs. Beat the yolks until thick and lemon colored. Beat in the sugar gradually.
Sift flour and salt together, then add alternately with the citrus juice to the first mixture.
Beat egg whites until foamy. Add baking powder and continue beating until they hold a point.

Fold into egg yolk mixture. Pour into an ungreased aluminum angel food pan.
Bake at 350° for one hour or until toothpick inserted into cake is dry.
Hang upside down on wine bottle until cool.

I n our family, these butter cookies were called Fannies, because they came from Aunt Fanny's recipe collection. I can remember baking these cookies with my mother from the time I can remember anything at all. It was a ritual, maybe two or three times a week. She would give me a blob of dough and I'd make all sorts of shapes with it. By the time I was 7, I could make the same perfect circles she did.

Now, having made these cookies thousands and thousands of times, I could do it blindfolded. One thing that always struck me growing up is why my mother called them butter cookies – after all, she made them with Crisco. She explained that the butter shortage during World War II necessitated alternatives. So, one day I suggested we try the recipe with butter. And guess what? They were even better than the Crisco version, and we've been making them that way ever since. My Mom died in 1997 and every time I make these cookies I think of her. I always keep a few dozen in the freezer.

–From her daughter Ronnie Fein

Lily Vail's "Fannies"

1/2 lb unsalted butter cut into chunks
1/2 cup sugar
2 cups all-purpose flour
2 egg yolks
1/2 tsp salt
1 tsp vanilla extract
1 can or jar apricot lekvar (sometimes called apricot butter or cake filling)

Preheat the oven to 350°. Beat the butter and sugar in the bowl of an electric mixer set at moderate speed for about one minute, or until well blended. Add the flour and beat for another 1-2 minutes, or until it is almost incorporated. Add the egg yolks, salt and vanilla extract and beat until uniformly colored dough forms.

Scrape the sides of the bowl, if necessary. Take off pieces of dough and shape them into balls about 1" in diameter. Flatten the balls, then make an indentation in the center with your thumb or index finger. Place the cookies on a cookie sheet, leaving about 1" between each. Fill the thumbprints with some of the apricot mixture. Bake about 25 minutes or until they are lightly browned. Makes about 5 dozen

When my mother gave a party, you could count on it being featured in our hometown newspaper. She loved to plan these events around a theme. One day, my dad came home announcing that he'd invited people over for brunch the next day. In a flash we were driving to the fabric store so she could make harmonizing tablecloths. As I recall, she served her delicious shrimp and artichoke casserole, and carved watermelons into baskets and filled them with fresh fruit. Then there was the time she decided to do a luau around the pool. She found authentic Hawaiian recipes, then called Dole Pineapple and asked them to send some of their 6-foot paper pineapples to our house. The guests were stunned!

When mom cooked for the family, everything was fresh, which was unusual for the 50's and 60's. She'd send me off to school with a sandwich on whole grain bread, fresh fruit and vegetables. All the other kids had Ho Ho's and Velveeta cheese sandwiches on Wonder Bread...I felt so deprived.

—From her son Scott Wilson

Beverly Kay Wilson's Shrimp and Artichoke Casserole

6 1/2 tbsp butter
4 1/2 tbsp flour
1 1/2 cups half & half
Salt and pepper
1/4 cup sherry
1 tbsp Worcestershire sauce
1/4 cup freshly grated Parmesan cheese
Paprika
1 #2 can or 1 pkg frozen artichoke hearts cooked according to directions
1 lb shrimp, cooked
1/2 lb fresh mushrooms

Preheat oven to 375°
Melt 4 1/2 tbsp butter and stir into flour. When blended, gradually add half & half, stirring constantly. When thickened, add salt and pepper to taste.
Arrange artichokes over bottom of buttered baking dish (8 x 10"). Scatter shrimp over artichokes. Saute mushrooms in remaining butter for 6 minutes. Spoon mushrooms over artichokes and shrimp.

Add sherry and Worcestershire sauce to cream sauce and pour over casserole. Sprinkle with Parmesan cheese and paprika. Bake 25-35 minutes.

There are certain aromas that awaken my childhood memories. The fragrant herbs and spices my mother used in her traditional Persian recipes would hit my nose and make my mouth water. I'd stand in the doorway, inhale the intoxicating aromas, and plot ways to get into the kitchen to steal a taste. Growing up around Middle Eastern culture, I could barely pronounce the names of most of these dishes, let alone imagine what potions or elixirs were added to the pot to make them taste and smell so

good. My mother always took great pleasure in creating these exotic meals for large groups of friends and family that would visit our home.

As a youngster, I abstained from almost anything that was inherently good for me. But Mom figured out that if you overwhelm the senses of taste and smell, a child won't realize that he/she just ate (GULP) spinach.

—From her daughter Doris Raymond

Mehri Ettehadieh's Eggplant Kuku

4 medium eggplants

1/3 cup vegetable oil

1 tsp salt

1/2 tsp pepper

1/4 tsp ground saffron dissolved in 1 tbsp hot water

4 cloves garlic, peeled and crushed

2 medium onions, peeled and thinly sliced

4 eggs, separated

3 tbsp lemon juice

2 tbsp butter

4 tbsp chopped fresh parsley

1/2 cup chopped fresh spinach

Peel the eggplants then cut them lengthwise and saute in the oil until golden brown.
Add garlic in the last minutes of saute. While the eggplant cools, heat 3 tablespoons oil in a skillet over medium heat and add the onions. Stir until onions are translucent. Put the sauteed eggplants in a bowl and mash them. Add the chopped spinach and parsley. Preheat the oven to 350°.

Melt butter in an 8 or 9 inch baking dish. Beat the eggs whites until foamy and fold in the yolks.
Add salt, pepper, lemon and saffron and beat thoroughly. Fold this mixture into the eggplant and pour it into the baking dish. Bake about 45 minutes. Serve topped with plain yogurt or feta cheese.

When I was a child growing up in North Hollywood, California in the 1930's and 40's my grandparents lived with us. My grandmother was born in a small hill town near Parma, Italy in the late 1800's. She was an absolutely marvelous cook and I learned my love of cooking from her. I would sit on a high stool while Grandmother let me help her shell peas or cut her homemade pasta. But when she made chocolate pudding, I think I spent more time licking the spoon than actually helping.

Grandmother rarely used formal written recipes, most of the time she just cooked by instinct. I have fond memories of being with her in the kitchen with all of the wonderful sights and smells. To this day, I love to cook and I often improvise on existing recipes using techniques I learned from her. On Thanksgiving and Christmas she always made this wonderful turkey stuffing. I made it for my family, and today my seven adult children use her recipe for their turkeys, too.

—From her grandson Richard D'Agostino

Josephine Colombo's Turkey Stuffing

2 loaves day-old bread

2 cups chopped onions

3 cups chopped celery

2 cups chopped mushrooms

Butter

2 lbs pork sausage (bulk)

1 cup chopped parsley

2 to 3 cups chicken broth

1 cup slivered almonds

1 tbsp poultry seasoning

Fresh sage to taste, chopped

Salt and pepper to taste

Saute the onions, celery and mushrooms in butter until the onions are translucent. In a separate pan, crumble and brown the sausage. Bring the chicken broth to a slow boil and let simmer. Cut the bread into small cubes. Add the cooked onions, celery, mushrooms, sausage and enough of the hot chicken broth to the desired degree of moistness. Mix well.

Add the parsley, almonds, sage, poultry seasoning, salt and pepper. Mix well.
Stuff both cavities of the turkey.

When I tell people that I spent part of my early childhood in public housing in New Jersey, it may not seem like a happy childhood to them. But for my sister, three brothers and me, it was great. There was always someone to play with, and my mother's parents and 11 siblings lived in the neighboring towns.

Money was tight, but we always had food on the table. Sometimes, when there wasn't enough money to go to the market, our meals were based on whatever was in the house, and my mother had to be very creative. Even though meals during the week were often light (meaning no seconds), on Sundays we always had an excellent dinner. There was meat, two different types of vegetables, rolls and, of course, the most exciting part of the meal…dessert.

When my mother prepared her Old Fashioned Gingerbread, the five of us couldn't wait until it came from the oven so that we could get our piece and smother it with butter. Or we would try to wait patiently while it cooled and then we'd drown the gingerbread with whipped cream and enjoy a piece of heaven.

—*From her daughter Vicki Anderson*

Thelma A. Parks' Old Fashioned Gingerbread

1/2 cup butter or margarine
1/2 cup sugar
1 egg
2 1/2 cups flour
1 1/2 tsp baking soda
1 tsp cinnamon

1 tsp ginger
1/2 tsp ground cloves
1/2 tsp salt
1 cup molasses
1 cup hot water

Pre-heat oven to 350°

Thoroughly grease an oblong pan.

Combine flour, baking soda, cinnamon, ginger, cloves and salt, and set aside.

In a large bowl, combine butter, sugar and egg, mix thoroughly.

Add dry ingredients, alternately add molasses and hot water mixture and pour in pan.

Bake 1 hour and 15 minutes, or until cake springs back when lightly touched.

Serve with whipped cream when cooled.

Nothing could take the chill off those long Connecticut winters faster than the Italian home cooking I grew up on. As with most families, our holiday celebrations centered around food. I remember vividly Christmas at my grandmother's house, her table laden with plates, silverware, and serving bowls of every description.

My mother and her four sisters would gather in the kitchen planning the details of this grand feast that would last for hours. Each of my aunts prepared a special dish, but the meal usually started with my mother's heartwarming soup with tiny meatballs, always made with laughter and love.

Looking back, I realize these family gatherings fed the dreams of my generation. I hope you will enjoy this recipe as much as I do and share a little of that moment in time.

—From her son Joseph Loconto

Edith Loconto's Soup With Tiny Meatballs & Escarole

Meatballs:
1/2 lb chopped beef
2 tbsp grated Romano cheese
Small slice Italian bread soaked in water, squeezed dry
1 egg
Dash of salt and pepper
2 tsp chopped parsley
Mix ingredients together and shape into meatballs, about the size of large grapes.

Soup:
2 heads escarole
6 cups home made chicken broth
Grated Parmesan cheese

Cut escarole leaves from root end and wash well. Drain and cut roughly into 1" strips.
Bring pot of water to boil, add salt and escarole. Blanch escarole for 2-3 minutes.
Drain and squeeze out water. Bring broth to boil. Add meatballs and chopped escarole.
Reduce heat and cook gently about 7-8 minutes.
Serve with a generous sprinkle of Parmesan cheese. Serves 4-6

This recipe started with my grandmother, who passed it on to my mother…who passed it on to me…and of course I continued the tradition by passing it on to my daughters. My grandchildren love this delightful dish, and they expect me to serve it at all our family celebrations. As I mix the ingredients I find myself humming the same tune my mother sang softly, as she prepared the kugel for our table.

Like many women of her era, my mother rarely had written recipes for her signature dishes. Over the years I have estimated quantities and tried to duplicate the luscious tastes she created. When mom cooked, she dressed in high-heeled shoes, stockings, colorful dresses and earrings. We always knew when she was about to spend time in the kitchen by the brightly colored, perfectly pressed apron tied at her waist. Now, whenever I make the kugel I think how pleased my mother would be to know that her recipe is bringing joy to the next generation

—From her daughter Susan Dechter

Sally Dechter's Noodle Kugel

12 oz package wide egg noodles
1 small container large curd cottage cheese
1 small container sour cream
1 stick butter, melted
3 eggs
1 tsp sugar
Optional: raisins, apples, jam or dried fruit

Boil the noodles until soft. Add all other ingredients and mix well. Place in a buttered rectangular glass baking dish. Bake at 350° for 1 hour or until firm. Serve hot or cold.

When I was growing up, we always had our big meal at mid-day, so Mama would pick me up at school and bring me home for lunch, even when I was in high school. Most days, the menu included one of her wonderful homemade soups. She'd use everything in the kitchen to create these delicious, nourishing and economical meals for the family. (This woman could stretch a chicken for a week!). Mama, who recently celebrated her 100th birthday, made this soup whenever we had a "Texas blue norther," a major cold front that can lower the temperature by 30 degrees in a couple of hours.

I'm sure my grandmother, who lived to be 96, taught her this recipe. If there was no sausage or bacon, she made it without, and she'd skip the dill weed if there was none in the garden. I love to make this soup on a cold, rainy California day, and when I do, I usually drain the sauerkraut then add the juice to taste, and I go a little heavier on the caraway seed than Mama did, because I like the flavor.

—From her daughter Charlene Mikeska

Albina Mikeska's Sauerkraut and Potato Soup

4 1/2 cups water
4 medium potatoes, peeled and cubed
1/2 tsp salt
1/4 tsp caraway seed
1/2 lb smoked sausage links, cut up, or
2-3 strips bacon
1 16-oz can sauerkraut
1 medium onion, chopped fine
1 clove garlic, minced
1 tbsp fresh dill weed, finely chopped
1 cup sour cream
1 tbsp flour
Salt and pepper toste
Sugar, optional

If you use bacon, crisply fry the bits in a heavy soup pot, drain off the grease, then combine water, potatoes and salt. Bring to boil and cook until tender. If you're using sausage, add it now with the sauerkraut, onion, garlic, dill and caraway. Bring to boil. Reduce heat and simmer about one hour. Combine cream with flour in small bowl and mix well. Add to soup, blend well. Heat thoroughly but do not boil. Season to taste with salt and pepper. If a less tart flavor is desired, add one tsp. sugar or less sauerkraut juice. Serve with dark bread.

We were a busy and active family but mealtimes, especially Sunday noon dinners, were a special time of togetherness for us. The menu was traditional American fare—along with the meat, potatoes, vegetables, relishes, jams, jellies and rolls there was always a special dessert. Most often there were family and friends to share these warm and happy times with us.

Our parents were always up early, way before time to leave for church. Mother prepared everything that could be done in advance, getting the roast into the oven and timing everything perfectly. As we left the house, one would never have guessed that this beautifully groomed, vivacious but calm lady had just prepared nearly the whole dinner. Within half an hour of arriving home from church, we were seated with the food arrayed in front of us, our parents handsomely hosting from the head and foot of the table. We remember the sparkling linens, Fostoria dinnerware, Wallace Rose Point silverware, and Mother's crisp white apron with its pressed handkerchief in the pocket. Our parents left an unforgettable legacy of warm friendship and care to all who knew them.

—From her daughters Judith Ulug and Becky Lourey

Alice Savage's Creamed Corn Casserole

2 14-oz cans creamed corn
1 cup soda crackers, crushed
1 egg
1/2 cup milk
1 tbsp flour
1 tbsp butter
1 tsp garlic salt
1 tsp cracked pepper

Melt the butter, add flour, garlic salt, pepper and milk. Cool until thick.
Add the corn, egg and crushed crackers.
Bake for one hour at 350°.

As a child, I lived for one glorious year with my grandmother, Gwen Andrews, in Chattanooga, Tennessee. Somehow, despite what must have been absolute chaos in the mornings, my grandmother managed to have a hot breakfast for ten on the table every day. Dinners were often prepared the night before and finished up just before serving. My favorite was what I came to call the

24-hour ham. Not only was it delicious for dinner, but it also made terrific sandwiches the next day with my grandmother's special homemade mayonnaise.

In the late 1960's, when her youngest child left home, my grandmother went back to school and became a Registered Nurse. She was 60 years old when she graduated (first in her class) and had been raising children for 40 years. She continued working as a nurse into her 80's. The girls in my family didn't need Women's Lib to tell us no one could stop us from accomplishing our dreams, we had Grandma.

—From her granddaughter Ginny Walters

Gwen Andrews' Twenty-Four Hour Ham

6-8 lb smoked ham shank
1/4 cup prepared mustard
1/2 cup brown sugar

Place the ham in a Dutch oven or covered stock pot. Cover entire ham with water and let sit overnight. In the morning, pour off the water. Place ham on a sheet of aluminum foil. Spread mustard on top and sprinkle with brown sugar. Wrap tightly in aluminum foil. Place in large Dutch oven. Bake, covered, at 250° for 10-12 hours.

Mayonnaise:
3 large egg yolks
3 tbsp lemon juice
1 1/2 cups oil
Salt and white pepper to taste

Using a free-standing mixer or a blender, lightly beat the yolks, then add the oil a few drops at a time, mixing constantly. When you've added half the oil, mix in the lemon juice. Slowly add the remaining oil, continuing to beat, until mayonnaise is fluffy and creamy. Season to taste with a pinch of salt and freshly ground white pepper. Refrigerate for a few hours before using.

I have such wonderful memories of coming home from school to find the house filled with the sweet aroma of these rolls. Not only did I love to eat them, but they signaled the fact that something special was about to happen...a holiday...special guests...or an important event. And, since things were always made fresh...certainly not frozen...whatever event was heralded by the sweet rolls was going to happen soon.

Sometimes my mother (shown right) made the rolls when I was home and then I got to help. I stood next to her, wearing a special apron my grandmother had made for me with my name embroidered on it in red. My job was to transfer the filled, rolled and cut dough into the baking pans. Much later I was "promoted" and allowed to spread on the filling.

Once the rolls went into the oven I would sit at the kitchen table with a book and wait for the timer to go off. My efforts were always rewarded with a delicious hot roll.

—*From her daughter Rivel Greenberg*

Mary Mondschain's Sweet Rolls

1 cup milk
1 stick butter
4 cups flour
2 tsp sugar
1 pkg dry yeast
1/2 cup sugar

1/2 tsp salt
2 eggs, well beaten
Grated rind and juice of one large orange
3/4 cup sugar
3/4 stick butter, melted

Bring the milk and stick of butter to a slight boil, stirring constantly. Remove from heat and set aside. Put the flour in a large mixing bowl. Make a well in the center and add 2 tsp sugar. Dissolve the yeast in 1/4 cup of warm water. Pour the yeast mixture over the sugar and let stand for 10 minutes.

In another bowl, mix together 1/2 cup sugar, the salt and eggs. Beat well then pour over flour. Add the warm milk/butter mixture. Mix all together. Cover and refrigerate overnight.

Mix together 3/4 cup sugar, orange rind and juice. Set aside. Place dough on well-floured board and knead until it is easy to handle, adding a little flour if it is sticky. Divide dough into 3 parts. With your hands, roll each section into a rope and then with a rolling pin roll the rope into a rectangle approx. 18" x 8". Brush dough with melted butter then sprinkle with 1/3 of the sugar and orange mixture. Starting at the bottom of the rectangle, roll the dough up and cut it into 12 sections. Place each in a well-greased muffin pan. Cover pans with a towel and let them sit at room temperature for about an hour, or until approximately doubled in size. Bake at 350° for 25-35 minutes.

When I was growing up we had chicken for dinner every Sunday, and it was always "free range" from our backyard. My mother, Eva Marie, was of French descent and a marvelous cook. Her oven-fried chicken was one of my favorites. Along with the chicken she'd serve her heavenly mashed potatoes with gravy and vegetables, all from my dad's garden. She usually had a wonderful pie in the oven (her most memorable was banana cream), and homemade bread. My father, Raymond, owned the flour mill and grain elevator in town, so she didn't have far to go to get the flour she needed.

I hope when you make this dish, it's as delicious as the one I remember from my childhood in the small village of Bowlus, Minnesota, where Eva and Ray raised their seven children.

—*From her daughter Katherine Sobieck*

Eva Richard Sobieck's Sunday Chicken

1 whole free range chicken, cut into pieces
2 cups white flour
Salt & pepper to taste
Lawry's Seasoning to taste
Mazola Oil (or substitute olive oil)

In a paper bag, combine flour and seasoning.
Shake chicken pieces in the bag until well coated.

Heat the oil in a large skillet and brown the chicken evenly.
Transfer to a Dutch oven and bake in 350° oven for 45 minutes to 1 hour.
The chicken should almost be falling away from the bone.

Feeding her family was probably my mother's number one priority…that and insuring that my brother and I get a college education. She, indeed, nourished us in many ways. I cannot recall when my mom didn't work. She was a legal secretary and in those years, during the 50s and 60s, considered herself a "liberated" woman. She spent each Sunday preparing the week's meals and freezing them. Neither take-out nor eating out were options.

It's not surprising, then, that any holiday when she was home was special to me. Thanksgiving in particular brings back my warmest memories. My mother made a dessert she called "parfait" pie. It was the perfect complement to the traditionally heavy dishes consumed during the meal itself. It was light, pleasing to the eye, easy to make, and so, so good. But best of all was that she and I prepared it together, our only chance in those hectic years to share a culinary experience. Those moments spent with my mother in the kitchen are among my most cherished memories.

—From her daughter Charlotte Gordon

Ida Goldstein's Holiday Parfait Pie

1 3 oz package red Jello
1 cup boiling water
1 pint vanilla ice cream
1 30 oz can fruit cocktail or sliced peaches
1 9 inch prepared pie crust
Whipped cream (optional)

Prepare pie crust per package instructions. Let cool.
(Or you can make your own crust as my mother did.)

Empty Jello into a bowl. Dissolve with one cup boiling water.
Spoon ice cream into dissolved Jello and stir until melted.
Place bowl in freezer compartment of refrigerator until mixture thickens (20 minutes).
Drain canned fruit thoroughly. Discard juice.
Add about 3/4 of the fruit to the thickened Jello/ice cream mixture.
Return mixture to freezer for further jelling (about 20 minutes).

Using a spoon or a spatula, spread the mixture into the cooled pie crust. Garnish the top
with the remaining fruit. Place in freezer for 20 minutes then transfer to refrigerator.
Serve with a dollop of whipped cream.

When my sisters and I thought about which of Mom's recipes we'd like to see published we agreed, hands down, that it would be her delicious Spring Cake. Although she made it year 'round, mostly, we associate it with the first strawberries of the season. There was nothing better. Mom was an artist in many ways. She painted, stitched, gardened and cooked with immense talent and enthusiasm. She took great pleasure in planning her meals and she always seemed to know exactly what was needed in the way of spices and herbs to make the dish special. She had a big, black cast iron pot that was used for almost every meal.

I remember coming home from school to find that big pot heating up on the stove, usually with a little oil in it, and mom chopping something...it didn't matter what because we knew the end result would be wonderful. Soon those fabulous aromas would fill the house and we could hardly wait to hear her call, "dinner time!"

—From her daughter Mary Ann Ross

Martha McKilop's Spring Cake with Strawberries

1 cup white sugar
4 eggs, separated
4 tbsp water
1 tsp vinegar
1 cup flour, sifted
1 tsp baking powder
1 tsp vanilla
Fresh strawberries in season

Beat egg yolks and combine with sugar. Add the water and vinegar.
Blend in the flour, baking powder and vanilla.
Beat egg whites until stiff and fold into the above mixture carefully.
Pour into angel food cake pan.
Bake at 350° about 1/2 hour. Hang over a bottle to cool.

Serve with sliced strawberries.

When I took my then 9-year-old son to see "On Golden Pond," he clutched my hand tightly as the movie unfolded and then excitedly shouted, "It's grandma and grandpa!" And in a way, it was.

After clearing the land, my parents built their dream cabin at the lake, where we spent many wonderful summers, swimming, fishing and fending off Minnesota mosquitoes. In the kitchen, my mother would pour over recipes, then set about producing savory meals that were always served on time—lunch at noon and supper at five. Sweets were usually baking in the oven for expected company.

One of our favorite dishes was her wild rice casserole. My father took out the canoe, pole in hand, and harvested the rice from a nearby lake, alongside the more skillful Indians. The recipe was rich with wild mushrooms they had picked (and we nervously ate), served with walleyed pike caught from the dock.

—From her daughter Beth Dahl

Jessie Johnson's Wild Rice Casserole

1 1/4 cups wild rice
Butter
1 can consommé
1/2 cup chopped parsley
1/2 cup chopped scallions
1 cup diagonally diced celery
1 1/2 cups boiling water
1 tsp salt
1/2 tsp dried marjoram
1/2 cup dry sherry
Mushrooms

Wash rice well and let stand an hour, covered with water. Drain thoroughly.
Melt some butter in medium casserole and lightly sauté the parsley, scallions and celery.
Add the rice, consommé, water, salt and marjoram. Cover and bake at 300°for 45 minutes
or until rice is tender and liquid absorbed. Stir with a fork 3 or 4 times. Stir in sherry
and bake 5 minutes more. Serves 8.

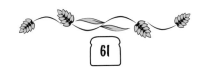

I spent every summer since I was 7 years old at my grandparents' home in a little French village near Nancy, called Blainville. My grandparents had a big vegetable garden, fruit trees, chickens and rabbits. Grandmother would be canning food for the winter months with all those vegetables and fruit. My memories are always about food because she would spend most of the day in the kitchen, cooking and preparing.

Quiche Lorraine was served on Sundays as a starter before lunch. When I came back from church my grandmother would take the quiche out of the oven and let it sit until we were ready to eat. The eggs used were from their chickens and the cream was from the farm down the road. Every time I make this recipe it takes me back to all the wonderful summer memories of my childhood. When I close my eyes I can actually smell the Quiche Lorraine baking in my grandmère's kitchen.

—From her granddaughter Beatrice Fort-Newhall

Marguerite Fort's Quiche Lorraine

Combine these ingredients and let settle:

3 eggs

1 1/2 cups cream

1/2 tsp salt

Pinch of pepper

Pinch of nutmeg

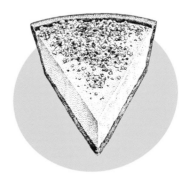

Sauté all these ingredients:

1 tbsp unsalted butter

1/4 cup chopped onions

1/3 cup sherry

1/4 cup chopped bacon

1/2 cup chopped parsley

1/8 cup thyme

3 cups Gruyere cheese, grated

9" pie crust

Spread cheese evenly in the pie crust. Add sautéed ingredients
then add strained custard mixture. Bake at 400° for 20 minutes.
Serves 4-5.

During the late 1950's my mother was always on the go volunteering at my school, at the local hospital guild, and on church committees as well as hosting the neighbors for morning coffees. She had a happy, traditional marriage to my wonderful dad, a man who wouldn't think of his wife working outside the home, so she kept her creative talents busy with volunteer work.

I have fond memories of her picking me up from school and off we'd go for an adventure in our 1956 turquoise and white Chevy. Mom made any project exciting and taught me many lessons in organizing, in coordinating people, and in finding fun and fulfillment in tasks I took on. After our errands, we would zoom home and dash into the kitchen where she'd throw together this quick casserole. My jobs were crushing the potato chips and setting the table.

My mother is now 74 years old and the executive manager of a small business. She started her career late in life but maintains the same enthusiasm and zest for new adventures as she did in her twenties.

—From her daughter Linda Scott

Dottie Smith's Potato Chip Tuna Casserole

1 can condensed cream of mushroom soup

1/3 cup milk

1 7-oz can of tuna

1 1/2 cups slightly crushed potato chips

Empty soup into 2-quart casserole dish. Add milk and stir until well mixed.

Add drained tuna. Put potato chips in plastic or paper bag. Crush slightly with rolling pin.

Measure 1 cup potato chips and stir into casserole. Sprinkle remaining chips on top.

Bake at 350° for 20 to 25 minutes. Serves 4.

My mom, Minnie Domino, a native Texan, has always known that in addition to praying together, a family that eats together stays together. Over the years she has juggled four children, career, grandchildren and a

plethora of church offices and responsibilities, yet she has always found the time to provide delicious meals for her family and friends.

When I was growing up, her Texas Succotash was usually on the menu for holidays, birthdays or any special occasion, and it's still my brother Warren's favorite dish. The wonderful tastes and smells emanating from my mother's kitchen on any given day are an undeniable reminder that although the day to day is ever changing, her love and provisions are constant.

—From her daughter Delorise Washington

Minnie Domino's Texas Succotash

1 1/2 lbs okra cut into 1/4" rounds
2 small yellow onions, chopped
1 16-oz can whole tomatoes, chopped
2 ears fresh corn or
1 16-oz. can whole kernal corn
2 tsp vegetable oil
4 tsp water
Salt and pepper, to taste
Garlic powder

In a 12" skillet, sauté the onions in vegetable oil. When onions become translucent, add the okra and cook for about 5 minutes over medium heat. Add the tomatoes and corn.
Cook until liquid evaporates. Add water, cover and simmer over low heat until okra begins to melt.
Season to taste with salt and pepper and a dash of garlic powder.

Trying to learn how to cook at "my mother's knee" was an exercise in futility. While recipes give specific measurements, temperatures and times, my mom's approach was much more inventive than the printed word.

Pinches, smidgens, dashes, splashes and dabs were all used as descriptors when I quizzed her as to how much of any ingredient was being added. Cool, medium-hot and broil were as definitive as the temperature ranges got. The length of time needed for cooking after assembly was "until it is done." Ingredient substitutions only added to the variables possible. So study as I might, I found figuring out what magic she worked as she was creating our meals to be always just a little beyond my ability.

Little did I realize then that the secret to her good cooking lay in her imagination and joy in preparation, not in the text of cookbooks or clipped recipes. Not until my own son began to ask me how to fix his favorites did I find myself using the very same words my mom had shared with me.

—*From her daughter Anna-Wynne Drevers*

Julia-Jane Holley's Icebox Plum Pudding

1 pkg lemon Jello

2 cups hot water

3/4 cups cooked prunes, cut up

3/4 cups Grapenuts

3/4 cups pecans or walnuts, chopped

3/4 cups seeded raisins

1/2 cup brown sugar (scant)

1/2 tsp cinnamon

1/4 tsp cloves

1/4 cup lemon juice

Dissolve Jello in the hot water. Mix together all ingredients and refrigerate until it hardens. Serve with pudding sauce or whipped cream.

Mother used to make this whenever we hadn't been to a Chinese restaurant for too long, or whenever we had left-over meat, whichever came first. My father didn't like it much, but my sister and I did. She never wrote a recipe down, she demonstrated them for us.

Mother worked at the grocery store with my daddy, and during my adolescence, we lived on the other side of town from the store, so sometimes she'd leave a pot of chow mein in the fridge for me. After my sister got married and moved out, it became a special treat for mother and me. It's still one of my favorite comfort foods, and my daughter Sonya likes it, too.

—From her daughter Shelley Singer

Dorothy Singer's Minneapolis Chow Mein

Leftover pot roast or a pound of lean hamburger

A bunch of celery

A decent-sized onion

Soy sauce, lots.

Mushrooms, about a pound fresh or a #2 can

Molasses, about two tablespoons.

Butter or vegetable oil to saute, or just water in the pot (see below)

Cornstarch. 1/4 cup, maybe more, maybe less.

Fried chow mein noodles, the kind that come in a plastic bag.

Chop the celery and onion. You don't want any chunks bigger than an inch. Throw them in a skillet or dutch oven with a little oil or butter in the bottom—a couple tablespoons—and sauté. Or put enough water in with the vegetables to cook them. Add three or four good shakes of soy sauce and maybe a tablespoon of molasses. Stir. Bring it to a boil, cover the pot and simmer until the celery and onion are done.
Add the mushrooms and simmer until done, then add the leftover pot roast. If you're using hamburger, crumble and cook it gently, then stir it in.

Mix the cornstarch with enough water to make it liquid, then slowly pour the mixture into the chow mein, stirring gently. When the chow mein begins to thicken, let it cook a little before adding more. Be sure the chow mein is the consistency of medium thick pea soup. Put half a cup or so of fried noodles on each plate and pour chow mein over them. Serve with a scoop of white rice.

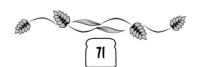

Growing up on a farm in Northwest Iowa in the 50's & 60's was truly a group effort. We all pitched in to make it a successful business, but I think my Mom worked the hardest. With five kids and a husband to care for, as well as doing farm chores, she rarely had a moment's rest. Mom had a huge garden, a large flock of chickens to tend, sewed most of our clothes, crocheted and quilted, canned and preserved veggies from the garden and flats of fruit, did laundry in a washtub with a wringer and hung the clothes outdoors during the summer. She was a great cook and baker, making nearly everything from scratch.

This recipe actually originated with Mrs. Thom, who taught my older siblings in a one-room country schoolhouse. When Mom made this Jello mold it was always a treat, as it used some ingredients that were deemed a bit extravagant in those days. Now, whenever I make it, I am immediately transported back 1500 miles and 35 years to our kitchen on the farm.

—From her daughter Marcia Rempell

Florence Dykstra's Orange Jello Mold

2 small packages orange Jello
1 cup boiling water
1 small can crushed pineapple, with juice
1 can Mandarin oranges, with juice
1 can frozen orange juice

Dissolve the Jello in boiling water. Let cool, but not set.
Add pineapple and Mandarin oranges with juice, frozen orange juice
and 3 (frozen o.j.) cans of water. Pour into a large ring mold.
Refrigerate until set.

I was named Laura for my Nonni (grandmother) who came from Sicily at the age of 16. When I married, my mother-in-law was named Laura, and when my daughter was born I named her Laura.

During the mid 1950's our family lived in the Washington Heights area of New York City where all the elders were from somewhere in Europe. Nonni Laura loved food and cooking and, of course, the opera live on the radio from the Metropolitan Opera House on Saturday afternoons. She would take me food shopping, first to Gatti's, the fruit and vegetable store where she would examine each piece with the eye of a surgeon and bargain for the best price. Then on to Irving, the butcher, where she would bargain some more. When we moved to New Jersey, we found there were no local specialty stores, just supermarkets. But my Nonni Laura had passed on her legacy to me, and then to my daughter—a love of food, cooking, and of course, bargaining.

The following is a recipe that my Nonni Laura made for me, I made for my children, and my children are now making for their children. Mangia bene!

–From her granddaughter Laura Manca

Nonni Laura's Pastina

6 oz pastina (according to Nonni—2 cupped handfuls)
2 qts water
Pat of butter
Pinch of salt
1 egg
Italian sauce
Parmegiana cheese

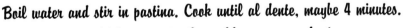

Boil water and stir in pastina. Cook until al dente, maybe 4 minutes.
Drain pastina, add butter, stir, then add raw egg and mix.
Add about 3 tbsp of sauce.

Sprinkle lots of Parmegiana cheese on top, and serve hot.

Long before your average family ate what we now refer to as "ethnic" food, my mother was experimenting with cuisines from other cultures. Just the thought of her Indian Chicken Tandoori still makes my mouth water. Preparation for this "company" feast began a full day in advance when mom would rub an exotic mixture of herbs and spices into the chicken and let it marinate overnight.

Curry is the primary flavor in this recipe, and to this very day the scent of curry conjures up all sorts of feelings: the excitement of company coming and the freedom that afforded us kids, and of course, the thought of leftovers. Mom would create an entire theme around this meal, dressing the table with a madras cloth, brass bells and candles placed on carved wooden trivets. The chicken was accompanied by white rice and condiments arrayed in Chinese teacups. After I was married, mom taught me her special techniques and now whenever I serve this dish these precious childhood memories come flooding back.

–From her daughter Jane Groner

Janet Cutler's Chicken Tandoori

2 broiler-fryer chickens, halved
2 large onions, chopped
2 green peppers, diced
2 tomatoes, chopped
2 tsp salt
1 tbsp curry powder
1 tbsp coriander

1 tbsp turmeric
1 tbsp ground cumin
1/2 tsp cinnamon
1/2 tsp black pepper
1/4 lb butter, melted
2 cups water

Place chicken in shallow baking pan. Combine seasonings and rub on chicken. Sprinkle with onions, green pepper and tomatoes. Pour melted butter over chicken. Turn chicken until mixed well with other ingredients. Cover and marinate for several hours or overnight. Before baking, add the water. Bake at 375° for 1 to 1 1/2 hours. Serves 4 to 6.

Serve with white rice and condiments: peanuts, chopped hard boiled eggs, chutney, grated coconut, raisins, thinly sliced green onions.

My mother was a terrific cook, but her baking is what I remember most. For family birthdays, she'd whip up a gorgeous layer cake with orange cream filling and frosting flecked with coconut and orange zest. Chocolate cake and banana cream pie were among her specialties, and there were always homemade cookies to nosh on. But lemon meringue pie was her signature dessert. The entire creation was made from scratch and it was as beautiful as it was delicious. The crust was always perfect, a skill I never mastered. The bright yellow filling was thick and tangy, and topping it off was a fluffy white meringue that stood about three inches high.

Mother made this special dessert whenever family and friends gathered at our house for dinner, even on Thanksgiving. And when it was her turn to entertain the card club, they were always treated to the lemon pie. Oh how I loved those ladies luncheons…I'd sneak down to the kitchen early the next morning before anyone was awake and help myself to a big slice of that lemon meringue pie, hoping she wouldn't notice it was gone.

—From her daughter Sally Leder

78

Dorothy Udell's Lemon Meringue Pie

7 level tbsp cornstarch
2 cups water
1 1/4 cups sugar
3 egg yolks, slightly beaten
Juice of 1 large lemon
Grated lemon rind
1 tbsp butter

For Meringue:

3-4 egg whites
6 tbsp sugar
1 tsp lemon juice

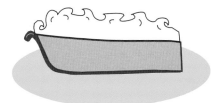

Baked 9" pie crust
Mix 1/2 cup water and cornstarch to a thin paste. Combine 1 1/2 cups water with the sugar in top part of double boiler. Boil for several minutes over direct heat. Add the cornstarch paste and cook until mixture thickens. Place the pan on the bottom portion of the double boiler and cook about 15 minutes.

Add a little of the mixture to the egg yolks, then return to the pot and cook another minute.
Remove from heat. Add lemon juice, grated rind, and butter. Cool, then pour into crust.

Beat the egg whites until stiff, adding sugar 1 tbsp at a time. Add lemon juice.
Spread the meringue lightly over cooled pie filling, bringing it to edges. Brown slightly in 325° oven.

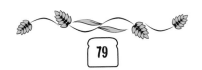

While my mother didn't have much talent for cooking, she worked hard at it. She collected recipes from friends, and meals were always beautifully presented on chintz patterned china and a freshly ironed tablecloth. She knew how to stretch a dollar, so that even when times were lean, we had an abundance of good things to eat. My lunch always included a raw carrot for my eyes. And after school there was a peanut butter and jelly sandwich and a glass of milk waiting for me.

Mid-day Sunday dinners were special with chicken, meat loaf or roast beef, mashed potatoes, green beans, salad, and her delicious lemon meringue pie or pound cake for dessert. Once a week, a local farmer came to town selling fresh produce door to door. With the apples he brought, my mother would make this wonderful Waldorf salad, a recipe she adapted from the Waldorf -Astoria Hotel in New York City.

After dinner, my sister and I played mathematical games in our heads, delaying as long as possible our job of washing the dishes.

—From her daughter Claudia Chapline

Stella Chapline's Waldorf Salad

4 stalks celery
3 apples
1/2 small package walnuts
1 tbsp mayonnaise
2 tbsp sugar
1/2 lb green seedless grapes
Pinch of salt

Chop the celery and walnuts. Cut apples into bite-size pieces, but don't peel.
Combine all ingredients in a medium-size bowl and toss. Arrange in a chilled glass bowl,
or chill overnight and serve the next day. Serves 4.

Y ou wouldn't think that kids could be so excited about dinner rolls, but my mom's rolls were truly special. She always made them for festive occasions, whether it was a luncheon for her lady friends or a family holiday dinner.

They were slightly sweet, and so delicious my sisters and I fought over them. Often mom would make an extra batch just to keep peace in the family.

Mother got the recipe from a friend of my grandmother whom we called Auntie Jo. I remember going to visit…we'd find her sitting on the big swing on the front porch, while a basket of fresh-baked rolls cooled in the kitchen. It seems that during the war, Auntie Jo's relatives used their food stamps to buy sugar and flour so they wouldn't be deprived of their favorite treat.

We still serve mother's rolls at every holiday dinner, a tradition that's continued for nearly 60 years. And whenever I make them, I use her original handwritten recipe, complete with the spots and splatters of a lifetime.

—From her daughter Donna Faulkner

Lefa Lynch's Dinner Rolls

2 yeast cakes
1 cup cold water
1 cup boiling water
1 cup shortening
2 eggs
3/4 cup sugar
6 cups flour
1 tsp salt
Butter

Break yeast in small pieces and soak in cold water while you prepare the rest. Pour boiling water over shortening and let cool. Then beat 2 whole eggs, add sugar, and yeast and cold water, and finally the flour which has been sifted 3 times with salt. Stir with a spoon then set in icebox. Three hours before baking, put in greased muffin tin, dropping 2 lumps the size of a marble in each cup. Put melted butter over rolls before putting in oven. Bake at 425° for 10 minutes, until golden brown.

Makes about 2 dozen.

My grandmother lived in Watsonville, California, in the Salinas Valley. She had a small bungalow on a postage stamp lot. Somehow she got chickens, a vegetable garden and fruit trees on it that provided the food for many a Sunday dinner. We would drive down Highway 1 in our big, blue, 8-year-old 1947 Dodge with my mother, father, aunt and uncle. Everything my grandmother made was great, but the special treat was always waiting…a warm plate of Grandmother's Cookies. It was a recipe, never written, that was passed down from her grandmother in Denmark.

When my mother became a grandmother, she started making them for family holidays, and when I became a grandmother, she passed the recipe on to me. Since grandmother measured by hand scoops, fists and pinches, my mother translated the recipe into standard measurements. I don't think you have to be a grandmother to bake these cookies, but it helps!

—From her granddaughter JoHanna Willmann

Sena Russell's Grandmother's Cookies

2 cups raisins
2 cups brown sugar
2 cups water
2 eggs, beaten
2 tbsp butter
3 cups flour
2 tsp baking powder
1 tsp soda
1 tsp each cinnamon & nutmeg
2 tbsp cocoa

1/4 tsp mace
1 cup chopped walnuts
1 tsp vanilla

For glaze:
3 tbsp water
2 tbsp corn syrup
1 tsp butter
2 1/2 to 3 cups powdered sugar

Combine raisins, brown sugar, water and eggs. Boil 10 minutes, add butter, and cool.
Sift together the flour, baking powder, soda, spices, mace and cocoa and add to above mixture.
Add nuts and vanilla. Spread on cookie sheets. Bake at 350° for 20 to 30 minutes.
Ice while warm with glaze, cut into bars when cool.

Glaze: Heat water, syrup and butter until butter melts. Remove from heat. Stir in powdered sugar
to thicken slightly. Beat until smooth.

My "Nonni" (grandmother) was the center of our large Italian family. Born in Palermo, Sicily, she immigrated to America at age four. Her father was a baker and her mother was known to cook for workmen who picked up their hot lunches from her kitchen, trattoria style. Our Sunday and holiday meals were always filled with "old world" recipes that were passed down through the generations. Aunt Dottie, my godmother, learned from her mother, my Nonni, in the kitchen where mothers and daughters (and sometimes sons, too) still gather in joy and love creating the food that fills our souls and warms our hearts.

Sfinciuni was often found in my grandmother's refrigerator and was a most welcomed snack when I was a young Catholic school girl, stopping off on my way home. Love was always deeply expressed with each food offering, and to this day, that same red carpet is rolled out for my visits, lined with the likes of pasta con sarde, rice balls, sfinciuni, and pastries. The heart of Sicily still beats gastronomically in our family!

–From her granddaughter Tina Villano Chase

Augustina Villano's Sfinciuni

2 1/2 lb pizza dough
Bread crumbs
1 package frozen artichokes steamed according to directions

Sauce:
1 1/2 lb onions, sliced the long way
1/2 can tomatoes
2 oz capers in brine, rinsed
1/2 can anchovies
Salt and pepper

Saute the onions, add tomatoes, capers and anchovies. Season to taste with salt and pepper.

Put pizza dough on oiled cookie sheet and flatten to 1/2" thick. Let it rise to 1" then imbed artichoke hearts into the dough. Put sauce, nice and thick, over the dough. Over this, sprinkle enough bread crumbs to cover. Should not be dry. Bake at 400° for 45 minutes.

My mother was born in Brooklyn, NY and was a lifelong Dodgers fan. Blessed with a wonderful outgoing personality, she loved to laugh and entertain friends and family. But most of all, she relished collecting recipes and trying them out on all of us. Once, she found a recipe for chicken cooked in Coca-Cola. Much to our surprise it was actually pretty good.

Like many women of her era, Mom didn't learn to cook at home. So after she was married and moved to Connecticut, she got pointers from her upstairs neighbor. Her Flank Steak recipe was served for company and special occasions. It only took her about an hour to make it, start to finish, but the rich aroma of pan-fried steak, caramelized onions and tomato sauce lasted in the kitchen for days. I can still remember how happy she was when my two brothers and I ate every morsel and became members of the clean plate club.

—*From her daughter Ellen Young*

Selma Young's Flank Steak in Wine Sauce

1 lb flank steak
1 tsp Kitchen Bouquet
2 tbsp oil
1/2 cup finely diced onion
8 oz can of tomato sauce
1/2 cup red wine
1/2 tsp salt
1/8 tsp pepper
1 1/2 tbsp corn starch
6 oz canned mushrooms

Cube the steak and coat with Kitchen Bouquet. Pour oil into a frying pan, add all the ingredients except the meat, and cook for about 5 minutes, or until onion is soft. Add steak and cook for 30 minutes. Serve over noodles, mashed potatoes or rice. Serves 6

How did she do it? There are times when I look back upon my mother's life in awe. She had five children, a home, a restaurant, employees, and all the strings attached. She fed us, clothed us, and the door was always open to our family and friends.

When life was hard, she made sure we had food on the table. When life was good, she threw great parties, lavish holidays, and gave extravagantly to all. At either end of the spectrum she put the needs of others first.

All of this during the pre-women's lib days, when single mothers typically had no help, no education, and no support system – she worked hard, educated herself, and combed the snarls out of my hair.

—*From her daughter Barbara Schora.*

Elizebeth Freeman Costa's Hermits

1/4 cup raisins or currants
1/4 cup chopped nuts
2 cups flour
4 tbsp butter
1/2 cup sugar
1/2 tsp salt
2 eggs

1/2 cup molasses
1 tsp baking soda
1/2 tsp cream of tartar
1 tsp cinnamon
1/2 tsp ground cloves
1/4 tsp mace
1/4 tsp nutmeg

Preheat oven to 350°

Grease a 9 "x 13" cake pan or cookie sheets. Toss raisins, currants and chopped nuts in 1/4 cup of flour, set aside. Cream the butter, then add sugar and blend well. Add salt, eggs, molasses and beat well. Mix in the remaining flour, baking soda, cream of tartar, cinnamon, cloves, mace and nutmeg. Add to butter and sugar mixture, beat thoroughly. Stir in raisins and nuts. Spread in the pan. Bake about 15-20 minutes, until the top is firm and the center chewy. Cut into squares. Makes about 36.

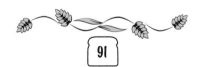

My Recipes

My Recipes

My Recipes